SCHOOL NIGHTS SOLO

SCHOOL NIGHTS SOLO

Tips for Single Parents on Education and Engagement

AVERY NIGHTINGALE

Creative Quill Press

CONTENTS

CHAPTER 1

Introduction

Transitioning from playtime at home to quiet reading in bed is rough. Kids want to keep up the fun, not stick their noses in a book before putting on their PJs. To tote academic learning over from school hours to bedtime, host a family book club. Gather books on a similar topic for everyone to read, or choose books by the same author. Once per week, meet and talk about one selected story while enjoying comfort food and family time. Everyone shares what they thought about the chosen story and listens to the opinions everyone else shares. This semi-formal meeting is much less intimidating than homework sessions and keeps the whole family connected to literature. Too quiet while reading in the other room to see what your kids are thinking? Share observations and open-ended questions as your child shuffles through their book to prompt deeper thinking.

Raising children as a single parent carries just as many challenges as joys. Balancing finances and spending quality time with children is difficult. Moreover, getting children settled into school and involved with their educations presents another struggle. As a single parent, you have no help in picture day preparations or class field trips. Even the most responsible and resourceful single parent struggles to keep every ball in the air. The educational involvement of a single parent often lands as low priority. However, follow these five easy tips for engagement under those harried circumstances. You only get one shot to set your children up with a lasting love of learning. So hit the books with these ideas to keep your kids connected to their educations, even on those cramped school nights.

CHAPTER 2

Establishing a Supportive Routine

After school, I have it more written down and nowhere else to go. To be honest, our after-school routine was not really discussed or established, but we could figure it out for the most part since then. Ty had time to either play outside or rest while spending time on his technology devices, or enjoy a snack while watching TV. His evening meals occur later than others because he wants it that way. With his daycare beginning tech time around 3:45 PM for the 1st and 2nd graders and outdoor time a little bit later, if he had to put down all electronics and eat dinner right away, he would not have a comfortable amount of time to play in the great outdoors "weather permitting" or have personal tech time. Also, if he has tech time while his mom prepares dinner, he is out of her hair which makes dinner preparations less stressful and quicker.

When it comes to a nightly routine, some single parents don't realize that they need one. At least in my case, the routine was right under my nose, I just didn't know to call it a routine and the structure was nonexistent. And structure for a nightly routine doesn't necessarily mean that everything was done in exact order every day. Structure can just be that we generally had dinner and then got ready for the next day, meaning all things that needed to be completed and/or needed attention ready to go. This general routine helps ease the stress that comes from anticipating an early morning rise, whether it be from an alarm, the sound of the school bus, or your child shaking you out of bed.

CHAPTER 3

Creating a Positive Learning Environment

Children will thrive with a routine that provides an orderly environment. Kids should not shop for shoes in a music store, do homework in the bathroom, or eat in the bedroom because they could not find a place in a rushed transition between dinner and homework. A consistent, child-friendly structure to the evenings means students feel queasy when the plan goes awry, a sure sign that the feeling of security your home offers encourages healthy, social, responsible behavior. A consistent and nurturing paradigm for daily living will also serve a parent well as he establishes his child's evening "job" as more serious than mere "discipline time" for academics, extracurricular activities, or the routine personal hygiene, pick-up-and-put-away chores. Such habits, established so late in the day, communicate powerful values that will resonate for the lifetime of your precious children.

Books on child development agree: Children learn best in a secure and loving environment. Herein lies a challenge for single parents. When our children spend the school week away from the family, the parents responsible for the primary relationship may feel guilty and bereft. Parents also worry that they will fall into the role, minimizing their child's effort, instead of encouraging independence and personal responsibility. Whether your children live with you full time or go to bed elsewhere is not the point because the activities described within these pages also hold true for non-custodial parents who see their children only on weekends. No matter where your children sleep, your home can become a valued venue for personal growth and academic success, whether or not the parent has a piano.

Effective Communication with Teachers

This is probably one of the top five areas of concern for everyone in our society. When parents get involved in their child's education, they are more likely to do well in school. It's challenging to find ways to stay involved due to jobs, other children, and sports activities. These are excuses that are almost impossible to keep up with. They are real life. They are also critical. You cannot always see hallways, lunchrooms, or classrooms due to your individual situation. This does not mean you can't get involved.

Effective communication between the teacher and the parent is crucial. Most teachers are open to helping a student achieve success. Keep the contacts from your student's teacher and use them as necessary. If this is not possible or you are not sure what this individual's office hours are, email is an alternative. I know what you're thinking. Email is the last form of communication that I'd expect a response from in a timely matter. It's true. However, if a teacher is able to send and receive email, there's a good chance that you'll create at least a comfortable line of communication.

CHAPTER 5

Encouraging Academic Success

2. Believe in the value of good grades. This is not about bragging rights. It's about using grades to identify what's working and what's not. As a parent, evaluate how engaged your child seems and how hard they are working. Then look at their report cards for clues of both strengths and improvement opportunities. Ask teachers about what your child seems to enjoy learning, their attitudes toward school, reading levels, efforts, or how you can help at home. Support your child in mastering the skills and staying on track. And provide loving pressure to meet objectives.

1. Positively acknowledge and reward children. Think about how you feel when someone gives you an unexpected compliment or simply a reassuring boost with a "You can do it." Research has found that the same simple acts of unexpected kindness can also positively affect children. Take the time to let your child know just how proud you are of them. Celebrate every

small success and encourage them to celebrate their friends as well. It is important for all kids to "feel good in school."

Here are five tips to help you encourage your child to become a successful student:

1. Make education a family value. 2. Make education a family affair (Get involved and stay involved). 3. Monitor progress and be a motivator. 4. Set the expectation high.

The love and support of a single parent can have a positive effect on a child's chance of academic success. Dr. John W. Rittinger, National Consultant for The Parent Institute, identifies four key areas where you, as a single parent, can provide this foundation for your child's academic achievement:

CHAPTER 6

Balancing Work and Parental Responsibilities

Let your boss know your status as a single parent. While we may want to keep our personal lives private, let's face it, being a single parent can affect our way of working, as well as responsibilities at work. Back to school nights usually involve listening to the teacher and taking this opportunity to meet with other parents. It's a wise idea to let your boss know the situation at work because it can be difficult for a single parent to attend some work-related activities. Tell your boss that the back to school night is the minimum that will allow you to participate in work or other acts. Although it is important to inform the boss of most of the requirements he makes of you, it is also important to bear in mind that you are a single parent who needs to balance family and work.

Many single parents, including single fathers and mothers, are pulled in the direction of work and other family members while trying to balance their time and resources to give their children the best they have. It can be stressful when it is time to help organize the homework and also try to bond with your children in those few hours in the evening. In this case, learn to say no and feel guilty. Many single parents, in an effort to repay their children for the lack of traditional family, give them everything they ask of them. Unfortunately, most children, left without a bid, will want more, more, and even more. You can help your children without giving them everything they ask for. In addition, children will learn the sense of values and others if they feel that they have responsibilities towards the house in which they are staying and that the landlord has the responsibility to consider the total family that lives in the house.

Building a Strong Relationship with Your Child

Children are different. Just because your child came out of you doesn't make you an expert in parenting him. Some children will never want to talk about what happens in their life. That is introversion. Other children calm down when they share. Shake off the image of the "80s parent" who was mean and made teens miserable. Friendship can possibly be the best thing to develop beyond infancy, with strict boundaries and a sense of safety, a balance between freedom and what is best for the teen. The friendship found in a good parent is an embryo of what the next generation will find as adults. I frequently tell my son that I am his mother first, always, and most of all. But we can have a friendship dynamic as long as we respect our roles. I do not allow anybody to call me things that are not respectful, so I wasn't going to allow my child to do that. I have to make sure that my child was not backward-thinking and that he was respectful and considerate to others.

Children thrive in a positive and caring environment. This may sound like a cliché, but time together is the key. Safe, relaxing, and loving quality time together is what your child needs the most. To help your child calm down after school, you might need to frequently organize calming activities. I am all for solitary play, but it is within our human nature to find comfort with others. Connection goes a long way in managing anxiety, worries, and stress.

"When the directions are wrong," said a 14-year-old student when I asked how he felt about adults, "I get agitated and mad! I like doing things right. If I'm doing something hard, I need somebody to praise me and show me that I'm doing something right."

There is no need for elaborate activities to build a strong relationship with your child. It is all about time spent together, giving encouragement and support, and lots of love and physical connections. Sometimes, an acknowledgement or a kind word or praise can make your child's day.

CHAPTER 8

Promoting Social and Emotional Development

Expectations in the home should be significant for one's child. Children, at an early age, need guidance and direction if they are to be successful and gain an understanding of the world. Expectations of academic success need to be set while a child of preschool age and established expectations for behavior in the home need to start then as well. The child needs to understand early on that they are not the only person with rights and responsibilities and know what is acceptable, what is not acceptable, and what the consequences will be for noncompliance or compliance. If an expectation of school achievement is established for the child, along with a home behavior plan, the child should have a strong foundation on which they can stand. Once parents and their children mutually accept the establishment of what is expected, children are more likely to be successful in both home and school while receiving support from home regardless of any hardships that may arise.

School-age children are beginning to move beyond their immediate family and into the world of friends and acquaintances. Social interactions and relationships among peers become more important. Friendships with peers are very close and important to school-age children. In addition, children at this age are learning to get along with others, learning consequences for their actions, and the rules of society. They are learning what is expected of them with regards to school achievement and rule enforcement for themselves and their peers. The rights and responsibilities for children will be applied at home and while in other environments such as school. With the implementation of a child's rights and responsibilities in the home setting, such should be developed in schools and within child inter-actions with their peers and adults in other community locations that they find themselves. The following are strategies to assist you with instilling social and emotional development in your children while instilling high expectations of education and expectations that are in the home.

CHAPTER 9

Nurturing a Love for Learning

Of all the academic achievement studies, which ones do you find more often in the closet? Why? GUIDATA and EXPLORE question once a day. For SCHOOL family night expose members of the family, no matter where they fall in the academic spectrum, to the incredible resources of knowledge available. School NJTs provide a welcoming environment for all of your child's families of origin: none, single, dual, grandmother, foster, half-siblings, etc. Remember, curiosity and creativity kill standardized evaluation design and therefore, are under constant attack these days.

Daily individual, intrinsic motivation can be ignited as quickly as it can be extinguished. Teaching methods that belie natural learning and acquisition motivations create activity but won't sustain motivation. Provide honest feedback; children can be more insightful, recognize our bias and act on it, better than newcomers to the language of instruction. To children's development needs, stereotypical school nights solo produce a systematic extinction of the two elemental ladders to academic achievement: curiosity and creativity.

Stuffed animals are not just for hospital rooms. If the reason behind the velvet rope around a stuffed animal or collector's craft is keeping it from getting dirty, put it behind glass. Watching a child's expression when the project they sweated over is used is worth a thousand wrinkled noses. Parents have to believe that they can have a say in how their child's classroom environment, including enriched curriculum (race cars, anyone?), is organized. It's possible to modify and influence through persistence without using the "A" word(s). It's also essential for other children to benefit from the rich, inviting environment. Interactivity for engaging social play challenges a single-child design. Reasonable conformity is an effective task rehearsal, preparation for the future.

CHAPTER 10

Managing Stress and Self-Care

It can be dangerous if parents forget to practice self-care. Caring for our physical and emotional needs is ongoing and essential. Illness in parents is concerning to children and can hijack a child's attention and focus on learning. Parents should model good self-care habits to ensure their children do not enter familiar patterns of neglect as they see such actions in parents. It is known that negligence can become generational. For instance, if children see their mother smoking, the chance for the children to grow up to be a smoker increases, with even greater probability if the mother smoked while the children were growing up. Stress can also increase the amount of cortisol a child produces. If caregiving males around a cortisone-producing woman mimic the woman in behavior, then they too (who already produce less cortisol than women) could overcorrect to do what they believe is best for the children and produce a dangerous amount of cortisol. Because privacy is limited due to the close living quarters, males could be under the impression that children don't see their form of stressful escape.

Frederick J. Stoddard, PhD, concluded, "That individuals after divorce or the death of a spouse have significantly more psychological distress than those who are married or happily coupled." He went on to write, "This distress keeps them from being fully involved with their children and can therefore hurt the children. The agony of paradox cannot allow a grief-stricken single mother or father to give his or her children the full attention and feelings they need." Coping tools can certainly help with psychological distress. Faith, friends, family members, and teachers are there for support and to remind us that we don't have to carry the weight and responsibility on our own. Additionally, these individuals can share personal advice and provide stress reduction techniques so children and parents continue to grow and thrive during their educational journey.

CHAPTER 11

Conclusion

The decision to stand on my own feet and raise my child on my own turned me into a square peg with a child who is now an adolescent with a system that continues to only fit round holes, but my son is way smarter and kinder than me, and turning him into a round peg is not my ultimate goal for him. His education is paramount, and yours should be for your child as well. You are enough for their education; you are maternal, my dear and inclusive fathers! I hope that I have been of some use to you, and as a single parent, I wish you the best of luck on your school journey, and remember: Take care of yourself.

I have been a single mother for most of my son's school years and have been the target of much well-meaning advice from friends, family, and acquaintances. Maybe some of this "advice" is actual helpful information that I'm too stubborn to see, but since I can only share what has been successful for me, with my son, I try to silence those with a slight smile and polite nod. Continue to do the same to me if my words seem of no use to you, but just stop reading after this sentence: Take care of yourself. If you do that, the rest will work itself out and fall into place.

9 798330 263516